YOU WITH HANDS
MORE INNOCENT

YOU WITH HANDS MORE INNOCENT

Selected Poems of Vesna Parun

Translated by Dasha C. Nisula

Art by Marko Marian

Publishers of Singular
Fiction, Poetry, Nonfiction, Translation, Drama and Graphic Books

Library and Archives Canada Cataloguing in Publication

Title: You with hands more innocent : selected poems of Vesna Parun /
  translated by Dasha C. Nisula ; art by Marko Marian.
Other titles: Poems. Selections (Green River Press). English I Selected
  poems of Vesna Parun.
Names: Parun, Vesna, author. I Nisula, Dasha Čulić, translator. I Marian,
  Marko, artist.
Description: New edition. I Poems translated from Croatian. I Previously
  published in Croatian with English translation under title: Selected poems
  of Vesna Parun. University Center, MI: Green River Press, ©1985. I Almost
  all of the poems in this book were selected from Šum krila, šum vode, edited
  with an afterword by Branko Maleš, Zagreb: Mladost, 1981. The last six
  poems are from the collection Stid me je umrijeti, selected and edited by
  Vlatko Pavletić, Zagreb: Mladost, 1989. I Includes bibliographical references.
Identifiers: Canadiana (print) 20190047852 I Canadiana (ebook)
  20190055057 I ISBN 9781550967296 (softcover) I
  ISBN 9781550967302 (EPUB) I ISBN 9781550967319 (Kindle) I
  ISBN 9781550967326 (PDF)
Classification: LCC PG1618.P26 A2 2019 I DDC 891.8/2154—dc23

Translation copyright © Dasha Čulić Nisula, 2019
Design and composition, and cover by Michael Callaghan
Typeset in Bembo and Birka fonts at Moons of Jupiter Studios
Published by Exile Editions Ltd ~ www.ExileEditions.com
144483 Southgate Road 14 – GD, Holstein, Ontario, N0G 2A0
Printed and Bound in Canada by Marquis

We gratefully acknowledge the Canada Council for the Arts, the Government
of Canada, the Ontario Arts Council, and the Ontario Media Development
Corporation for their support toward our publishing activities.

Canadian sales representation: The Canadian Manda Group, 664 Annette
Street, Toronto ON M6S 2C8 www.mandagroup.com 416 516 0911

North American and international distribution, and U.S. sales:
Independent Publishers Group, 814 North Franklin Street,
Chicago IL 60610 www.ipgbook.com toll free: 1 800 888 4741

For my parents,
Rose and Boris Čulić

CONTENTS

Introduction

How does one go about introducing Vesna Parun to a readership unfamiliar with Croatia and its literature? A relatively small country, the size of West Virginia, Croatia produces an inordinate number of poets, so many, one wonders what they are singing about all these years.

Vesna Parun is the first woman in Croatia who lived for and by writing, not only poetry, but prose, children's literature, and translations of poetry from Bulgarian, French, German, and Slovenian. Her own work had been translated into a dozen world languages. Then, one may ask, why is she not known outside her country? It appears that these translations have not been disseminated sufficiently to make her name one with her native land of Croatia, the country which today is the number one destination for many from Eastern and Western parts of Europe and America. And they all come not to read poetry but to share in what Croatian poets have been writing about all along: that beautiful landscape, the sun, nature, and the sea.

Five years after her death in 2010, interest in her work and life has been revived in 2015 by a powerful performance of Vesna Tominac Matačić in an emotional and intensive existential monodrama written by the poet and Ms. Matačić. The monodrama, *I, Who Have Hands More Innocent*, is produced by Tatjana Aćimović, and directed by Ivan Leo Lemo. The text was translated into English by Ellen Elias Bursać, while Parun's poems from Dasha Čulić Nisula's *Selected Poems of Vesna Parun* decorate the script. It has been performed in and outside of Croatia and in 2015 won the Grand Prix at the 17th International Monodrama Festival in Bitola, Macedonia. At the 2016 Fringe Festival in

Edinburgh, Scotland, the monodrama had a marathon run for the whole month of August with positive reviews. In one such review by Lucian Waugh, a contributor to the *Exeunt Magazine*, he bemoans that the translation of Parun's poetry is "maddeningly out-of-print." This new edition of the *Selected Poems of Vesna Parun* remedies the situation.

Vesna Parun made her debut with a book *Zore i vihori* (*Dawns and Hurricanes*) in 1947. The book appeared in print soon after the end of World War II. No one expected a book of poetry after the war to be full of life, optimism and expectations. What is interesting about the book is that it was and remains even today Vesna Parun's best work among the more than twenty books of poetry published during her lifetime.

What we have in her first book is an unadulterated voice pure, direct, and full of life, a fresh voice after a war that brought devastation to the country, families, and individuals. Yet, Vesna Parun's voice of hope and optimism was unfortunately not welcomed and encouraged by the critical establishment of the time. Instead, due to misunderstandings and shortsightedness, the critics attempted to crush the young woman's voice. It is possible that, as in words of Berislav Nikpalj, "she was more than beautiful, too smart, overly gifted, very proud and, on top of it all, too productive." And, in spite of everything that this poet endured during her lifetime, her voice and her determination to make it heard survived and endured. In fact, Parun was such a prolific writer, Karmen Milačić points out, she left a footprint in almost all literary forms.

A master of the classical form, especially the sonnet, which Parun says is her one and only tyrant, she is equally at home with free verse which by the end of World War II began to appear among a number of Croatian poets. What is most interesting about her work, perhaps leading to misunderstandings by the critics, is her non-traditional choice of subjects and manner of execution, without literary allusions to any classical works or other poets.

From the beginning she focused her poems on the everyday experiences of a person who writes and tries to survive. Her poetry is existential and relates to life experiences specifically from a woman's perspective. She goes beyond any prescribed or expected subject, avoiding traditional norms to go from the immediate present, linking one subject matter to another in the blink of an eye.

Though her language is simple, direct, and clear, her mind is preoccupied by religious and philosophical questions. Her thoughts remain, however, anchored to her native soil, the sea, the everyday, and the biographical. Parun transcends the literary, political, and social, and reaches the plateau of human values. For her, love is the most important and the only thing that makes us and keeps us human; love, which must exist if we are to preserve our humanity and the world.

The first place in her work is occupied by love, and in the second place is the sea - the only image she carries with her from her childhood on the island of Zlarin. Nature and her native land follow. But nature in Parun's poems is not just a static decoration, as Nikola Miličević writes. It is a testament to life which is dynamic, as everything in nature exists in some miraculous harmony and mutual support. Her love poems, of which there are many, are the most beautiful love poems ever written in the Croatian language. In reading Parun's love poems we become aware of the fact that – before her – love poetry focused on love of women as objects, while with Parun we learn more about love from a woman as a subject.

In addition to books of poetry, prose, dramatic pieces, and translations, her extensive contribution to literature for children won her an award. An updated list of honours and publications is included at the back of this edition. This still may not be the complete picture of everything Vesna Parun produced during her lifetime, as further works are yet to be discovered.

The second edition of *Selected Poems of Vesna Parun* consists of the same poems which appeared in the first edition, with some minor changes in the translated text. Because Vesna Parun was such a prolific writer, the bibliographical section has been expanded to include a separate list for juvenile literature.

Books Consulted

Bartolić, Zvonimir. "Jedan pogled na poeziju Vesne Parun," in *Sto soneta.* Čakovec: Zrinski, 1972, pp. 117-138.

Derk, Denis. "Neispunjene želje i ispunjen život," in Vesna Parun's *Ja koja imam nevinije ruke: asinkroni odabir,* 2nd ed., Zagreb: ZORO, 2010.

Lalić, Ivan V. "O poeziji Vesne Parun," in *O poeziji dvanaest pesnika.* Beograd: Slovo ljubve, 1980, pp. 88-102.

Maleš, Branko. "Kozmološki genetizam i naturalistički humanizam Vesne Parun," in *Šum krila, šum vode.* Zagreb: Mladost, 1981, pp. 197-214.

Mandić, Igor. "Umjesto pogovora," in *Jedna antologija hrvatske poratne poezije.* Zagreb: Znanje, 1987, pp. 283-287.

Milačić, Karmen. "Pjesničko djelo Vesne Parun," in *Izbor iz djela* Zagreb: Školska knjiga, 1995, pp. 5-22.

Miličević, Nikola. "Pjesnik i priroda," in *Poezija: Izbor.* Sarajevo: Veselin Masleša, 1988, pp. 196-197.

Nikpalj, Berislav. "Hod matere čovjekove," in *Stih: Journal of Poetry,* No. 2, Zagreb: August Cesarec, 1976, pp. 42-56.

Šoljan, Antun. "Tragična ćutilnost Vesne Parun," in *Poezija: Izbor.* Sarajevo: Veselin Masleša, 1988, pp. 5-13.

D.C.N.

"I came too early and too late to be a path of silence.
There is nothing for me but to sing.
To forever open my circle
and ruffle the unfinished world with my freedom."

Vesna Parun
Koralj vraćen moru, 1959

Dawns and Hurricanes

1947

I WAS A BOY

The evening, having turned off
the candles, hid me in the moonlight.
In the azure forest through the trees
I thoughtfully dreamt all night.

I was a grape from a red cluster
in the teeth amidst kisses
a fox that ran out of a snare
a boy, who throws shouts with a sling;

and a bite of a song in the middle of a forehead
a brindled cat in a play basket.
What haven't I been, what haven't I dared,
a mirror of a fish in the pupil of an otter!

A CHILD AND A MEADOW

Only a child clearly hears in the moss
the flutter of fast spring, the twitter in the feathers of the kingfisher.
It wanders after brooks, kisses juniper trees in the sun
while the eyes assume the colour of the nearby hill.

The child weaves the beauty of the morning with a smile
without paying attention to the permanence of some sound
spread by chance, in the wind.

Children are echoes of extinct things.
Bare and pure as a fish pond, they see themselves
in the face of the meadow, in the snare of the spider.

THE BODY AND SPRING

Put forth your leaves, my apple tree, the sun is at the door.
Secretly rises the brook and the wind roars from afar.
Noon warmly chirps, days are full of gold,
open the curtains, so I can look out at the azure sky.

Come to life with the whisper of a fruit, my quiet friend,
I will exchange with you, water well, for your clear eyes!
So the stone is my pillow, and my heart a goblet of colours
a soft bed of flowers where the bells madly ring.

Give me of your ancient song, world, turn me into a forest.
Let my soul put forth leaves, let it turn green in sleep.
I will exchange with the first one who tonight passes this way.
Spring is coming, listen: o mother, unveil my breasts!

WINDOWS

I dream of green ships in a quiet harbour
in an unknown region from the other side of the hill.
Somewhere, very far, a dog barks. A restless road waits
in front of the house. A horse with a golden mane neighs
in a walled-in yard. There is no wind.

If I climb to the tower, I will see a round sky
low, low clouds. One swallow and smoke of a ship.
Still further, the world will be spacious, strange.

Under a red balcony, the evening sleeps on the roses.

WAR

My grandfather sits in front of the house as the leaves are falling.
He looks at the figs drying on the rock
while the sun, very orange, sets behind a small vineyard
which I remember from my childhood.

My grandfather's voice is golden, it hums as some old clock
his speech is gloomy and full of restlessness.
The legend of seven hungry years comes right after the Our Father
it is short and endless.

But one day the fishing grounds became desolate.
There – it is now war.
The enemy besiege the harbour ten miles around
and the whole small island shakes in the eclipse.

Sons have long ago sailed the hard sea for bread
Canada
Australia…
Surely they will be taken on board for Japan.
Lucky if they are left somewhere alive among the bamboos.

Already the second winter ours incessantly move on foot.
A sullen pursuit is heard all the way to the quiet fish.
The grandson is good and blond. You will find him yet in snow
one day when the mountains become tired.

The maidens sing while cooking camp gruel.
The smallest ones squat on the floor in enormous fear

of the elegant officer's boot.
Mother thinks about the sons and the father, who became a Malay.

Strange,
what has scattered these people to all four corners of the world
these large heavy people who in their letters are so much like children?

My grandfather looks at the red sun behind the vineyard
quietly worried about death, the old navigator.

The foreigner is hunger. Freedom is a piece of bread.

Ah, tell the earth to turn the water-mills faster!
In rough weather the leaves have fallen; but what has to come
rightly, has to come.

There – boys are dying, and the old warm their grief
looking at the open sea.

THE GREEN FRAME OF DEATH

With a lowered face, one young woman in black
appeared quietly in the green frame.
A child caresses a cat. The window is open.
Who scattered the sun to the sparrows of childlike eyes?

The afternoon enters high up into the reddish hill, into the fruits,
and a child breathes in the green frame of death.
The woman, tired of mourning, of headache,
puts out the sun with her palm. She throws the day into the river.

The sparrows fly down and leave, without a care and unknown.
They gently love the orange autumn.
The woman is leaving without a smile. The child is playing.
The red flowers wither on the deserted window.

A horseman descends from the hill, through the trees.
From the woods gloominess accompanies the obscure rider.
Two turbid eyes: the stamping is closer.
The child presses its finger against the golden image and is silent.

The women in black are moving. Much blackness, many sad women.
The darkness grows, the cat meows in the window.
The footsteps are very close. Where is the child?
Who is touching grandmother's locked drawer?

The street is long; the street turns to the left.
The footsteps disappeared. They went around the house.
The green frame is silent; no one is crying.
The child's clenched fingers hang in partial shadow.

MOTHER OF MANKIND

It would have been better had you given birth to black winter, mother
    dear, than to me.
Had you given birth to a bear in a burrow, a snake on a log.
And had you kissed a stone, rather than my face,
it would have been better had I been nursed by the udder of a beast,
    than by a woman.

And had you given birth to a bird, mother dear, you would be a mother.
You would be happy, you would warm the bird under your wing.
If you had given birth to a tree, the tree would come to life in the
    spring,
the lime tree would blossom, from your song the reed would turn
    green.

By your feet a lamb would rest, had you been a mother to a lamb.
If you babble and cry, the kind beast would understand you.
This way, you stand alone and alone you share your stillness with the
    graves;
it is bitter to be a man, as long as man takes a knife for a friend.

THE BLACK OLIVE TREE
1955

MAIDENHOOD

That stamping and that smoke that is drawing nearer
will enter your garden, open the sleeping door.
You are alone in the house. What will you tell him, maiden,
this unknown man who wants to die
in your bare arms, what will you tell him?

You are alone in an empty deserted house
which is embraced by a fern. From your window
the sky is always the same, gentle and far.
Tired horsemen ride down the streets.

But someone wants to die in your gentle arms
that no one has lulled in the nights.
Someone yearns tonight to embrace, while dying,
your thin waist and untouched hair.

Look at the road, look along the water, along the extended evening:
someone was calling you secretly from the shore.
Drop your braids down your shoulders. Run
open-hearted; don't be afraid if you tremble.
Run, run! Don't ask who it is that moans
nor who follows your steps in the dark.

The gravediggers have already taken from the wrecked house
the glittering corals and golden canaries.
The stories dissipated in the stillness.

Don't cry: this is love. Go through tracklessness.
Instead of earrings, you will carry the weight of pain,
maiden, if you choose life!

FIRST LOVE

In the rustling grass near the crossroads
I sit with a restless heart and wait for him
to whom last night I gave, innocently,
the frightened bird of my love.

In the glowing red moon of the hill
the autumn is already entangled.
The calmness of the lake grows from half shadows.

What shall I do if the one to whom
I gave my heart doesn't come?
(I handed him the heart as a bird
without thinking anything, astonished.)

The whisper of the night reaches from the dark fields.
Oh, my heart! Do not listen to the murmur of the grass.
It will lead you to grief.
Look:
water is changeable.

And the birds depart far across the hill
after the cold sun.

A QUIET POEM

One evening the fog breathed into the candles,
and now we are quieter than ever, now it is autumn.
Autumn is beautiful, autumn is hidden in the clouds.
We are not sad because it is autumn, we are sad because autumn is
    beautiful.

The eyes are forever saying farewell, incessantly the eyes tear away
    from the horizon.
Dusks descend on the stillness of the leaves, dusks and doves.

Who will tomorrow walk the shore of quiet rivers?
Perhaps we haven't yet been anywhere, who will believe a heart!

One should cry a lot, for a long time one should cry silently
this strange autumn, stray night in the windows,
and our quiet lost hands.

My friend!
Look, and the autumn is already leaving, still and beautiful as a coral.

OLIVES, POMEGRANATES AND CLOUDS

When I meet him on the road, I turn my face after clouds
yet three days I waited by the fence for him to pass.
Since, pomegranates have begun to bloom, the sea has swelled.

How serious is the evening, and his eyes close in the stars.

He is so handsome in the black sky
sparkling as a shell.

But already I am tortured by what is to come.
For there: the wind rises from the cape of the olive-trees.
And this deserted naked heart
trembles and listens.

Already three days behind the fence, full of youth, I wait
for your steps among the dark olive trees.

A BALCONY

Two pins pinned to the curtain prolong the night
above the extended river across the path.
One little light appeared at the end of the yard.
Is this love walking, barefoot, in the moist flowers?

Once our hands together sought darkness
and the eyes caressed the wind calmed in passing
while we stood in the grass, so near the waves.

Now the evening is alone at the intersection,
now the shores of the eyes are desolate.
Only the wind goes down the winter road.

Two pins pinned to the curtain prolong the night.

A CAVE WITH A SPRING AND A FLOWER

Am I a recollection in the rock
or suffering in repose?

Many homeless come to me
who do not hear the seasons,
because in this forsaken place grows
only one nameless flower,
the mediator between you and the moon.
And it shows to the strayed
the traces of the ass in the sand,
and to the thirsty the crack
where the rock once long ago
had pity on the travellers.

They arrive here from four corners of the world
those who think they are unhappy,
and others equally wretched
who know not what to call happiness.

They drink. They rest
and they go onward, their shoulders bent
as if in conversation with a criminal.

And I am left again alone
and I look at these shadows as they disappear,
disturbing the horizon.

Some of them I forget immediately
but others I remember. They fill me
with a dark desire, inexplicably
vague as is the growth of a flower
in a trackless region between heaven and earth.

And while I think of them I become
even more barren and even more a cliff.
A recollection which consoles the rock
and suffering which cannot find rest.

HARBOUR

On the shore is a young woman; a scarf flutters in the wind.
But the ships do not approach the harbour; they go in their own
   direction.

A tired scene: two – three palm trees and an empty bench.
A sad face under the south wind, a yellow shore.

In the distance the towns light up; the woman is alone and nameless.
But the ships do not turn into the harbour; they sail off in their own
   direction.

The vine withers in the window; ancient songs are not being sung.
An unknown funeral approaches with a heavy tread.

The woman entered a tavern where a kerosene lamp sulks.
Life, a red torch, moves away in the distance.

OPENED DOOR

When the birds in the fall leave
their marshes, they whisper goodbye
to the bent and mute reeds
from which summer reflection is disappearing.

And tree parts with tree
in uneasiness and in sadness
resting their absent-minded branches
one upon the other, listening to the river.

But he opened the door of the cabin
looked at the sky and left
leaving a lit candle
near immobile books, and stillness
blurred with swaying thin shadows.

Oh night, transform him into a black rock
at the crossroads under the steep hill
from which the howl of the wolves descends to the sea!
Let leaves fall near him
hiding in their rustle
his unhappy loneliness.
And let the moon circumvent him
without gilding his edges
with the light with which it quiets the meadows.

Oh night, transform his heart into a flower
on the high hills of indifference
where my tears mixed with the saltiness
of the seaweeds can no longer reach.

Transform him into a cold island
with rugged and unwelcome shores
on which neither a stork nor
a silvery crane will descend.
Let the hurricanes from the north and the south
disturb his promontories
surrounded by the roar of the waves.
And everywhere around him
let the sadness of the sea spread
and despair and the everlasting contemplation.

I shall then close the door
and snuff out the tired candle.
The night will be very gentle
and it will not remember anything.

He will be unreal. Distance
will extend between him and me
as a nice friendly hand
which hides the devastation of the world.

IF YOU WERE NEAR

If you were near, I would lean my forehead against your walking
stick and, smiling, I would wrap my hands around your knees.
But you are not near, and my restless love for you
can sleep neither in the evening grass
nor on the ocean's wave, nor on the lilies.

If you were near. If you were at least so
inconstantly near as a rain cloud
above a lost house in the valley,
as a cry of a seagull that flies off above a pale sea
before the arrival of a storm on a care-laden evening.

Oh, if you were at least so sadly near
as a flower that sleeps with closed eyes
under the white cover of snow, in the silence
of rocky forests, waiting for spring.

If you were near, oh my cold flower.
With only one stir if you were near
my unhappy gardens
which already wither dejected by the vigil.

But it is night, and the world is far.
And I do not know your peace. Your birds
have flown off my branches. And the radiance of dawn
is departing forever from my pupils
into the offended land of the oblivion
in which the name of love is unknown.

YOU WITH HANDS MORE INNOCENT

You with hands more innocent than mine
and who are wise as the carefree.
You who are able to read the isolation
on his forehead better than I,
and who can lift lingering shadows
of hesitation off his face
as the spring wind removes
shadows of the cloud that float above the hill

If your embrace cheers up the heart
and your thighs stop the pain
if your name is peace
to his restless mind and your voice
a shade at his bedside
and a night of your voice an orchard
untouched by the storms

Then remain by his side
and be more devoted than all
who had loved him before you.
Fear the echoes that approach
innocent beds of love.
And be gentle to his sleep,
under the invisible mountain
at the edge of the sea that roars.

Walk by his beach. Let the saddened
dolphins meet you.
Roam in his forest. Friendly lizards

will not harm you.
And thirsty snakes which I tamed
will be meek before you.

Let the birds I warmed sing to you
in the nights sharp with frost.
Let the boy I saved from a spy
on a deserted road caress you.
Let the flowers I watered with my tears
fill you with their fragrance.

I did not reap the best years
of his manhood. I did not
take his offspring into my bosom
which was plundered at bazaars
by the gazes of herd drivers
and greedy robbers.

I will never take his children
by the hand. And the stories
I prepared for them long ago
I will perhaps tell crying
to the little ill-fated bears
left in a dark forest.

You with hands more innocent than mine,
be gentle to his sleep
which has remained pure.
But allow me to see
his face, as unknown years
descend upon him.

And tell me once in a while something about him
so I don't have to ask strangers
who wonder about me, and neighbours
who pity my patience.

You with hands more innocent than mine,
remain by his bedstead
and be gentle to his sleep!

LET US INTOXICATE THE COACHMAN
WHO DRIVES OUR DAYS

Stop for a moment,
you who drive the remains of my radiance
down the swift river!
The summer has faded
and coolness extends above the rocks.

Do not reproach my empty hands.
They are cautious as gravediggers
who put aside old songs
in favour of a solitary stone table under a linden tree
where silence is celebrated.

In vain you light fires in the hill,
in vain you call my flocks
scattered across the hillocks
in fear before the blunt trumpeting
of the one I loved more joyfully than you.

You cannot call them back.
Let them roam
on trampled meadows!
Do not reproach my lost days.
My years, sad sisters
of your discouraged youth.

Tonight one should be luxurious
like a garden of sunflowers, lush
like rain and beautiful like a lake,

so we delight these trees
in which the wings of dejected birds already
frighten the wavering sun.

You must demand much from me
so I accustom myself to your wishes
as to a forest and clouds.
You must tell me simple tales
so that your voice quiets my eyes
so that I no longer look back
into the strangeness of the past.

Look! Haven't we arrived yet
to that curve where the murmur
of the rapid water becomes uneasy!
Approach! The summer has faded
and coolness extends above the rocks.

This intersection
will not return again.
This is the marriage
between the pine tree and the lake.

Let us proceed, dear!

Let us intoxicate the coachman who drives our days
so he will not know where to our trail ascends
nor before which abyss the animated
black horses of love will stop.

Faithful to Otters

1957

NOON

In the uncut grass I lie supine, an aching maiden.
In uncut grass my heart, a warm swallow.

In golden clouds above the blue birch trees
my foolish heart travels and sings.

My rampant heart, a white hen-pigeon
Oh, if only I could be giving away bundles of happiness!

A CALL INTO THE SILENCE

My hands are a cottage of brushwood amidst swift waters.
All around is darkness and night. The clouds walk the earth.

Will you come to my quiet gardens, into the leaves, into the dreams
to lull with music my white fields, white flax?

The forest is subsiding, the wind is subsiding, the road is fading.
The mountain is alone. No one is coming. The yellow moon

sits by the shore, by the shore it waits the whole long evening.
But the river is dark, the river is deep. The river continues to flow.

THE EVENING STAR

Low in the sky the evening star shines.
The murmur of the summer still lingers in the valley.
It is night, and we are going along a deserted region
the glow of transience illuminates our path.

How silent is the sea in the distance!
Its endlessness is solitary.
Here somewhere near in the bent grasses
the voice of the cricket complains incessantly.

It is night, and we are going along a naked region.
Our youth sets behind a mountain.
A star extinguishes. The mountain, growing, shines.
Our path disappears in silence.

BEFORE THE SEA, AS BEFORE DEATH, I HAVE NO SECRET

If you seek the road to my soul
take me to the stormy sea.

There you will see my life revealed
as a demolished temple; my youth
a plateau enclosed by fig trees.
My thighs: ancient lament
because of which pagan gods
bend at their knees.

Before the sea, as before death, I have no secret.
The earth and the moon become my body.
Love transplants my thoughts
into the gardens of eternity.

AN EPITAPH TO ONE UNNAMED

I wish I were a crossroad in the lowlands.
Then I would know in which direction you rode off.
I wish I were a cliff, under which your horse will
one night neigh, stopped
by the reflection of the flames which approach
resembling herds of purplish buffalo,
Then I would reassure the rider
and with my shadow I would protect
his shadow at the foot of the mountain.

There is a solitary oak tree in the lowlands,
not far from it rises a spring.
There one morning you will arrive alone,
without a horse and without youth, with a heaviness in your chest.
You will lie under that branched-out tree
and look, at last completely carefree,
at how the stars have changed.

I wish I were the moon, which will then
when the night falls, take off your boots
asking whether the ground is cold
in autumn, under the heavy sky.
Then there will remain so little time
to ask something else about you.
Perhaps I will come to know the fear
which, growing, becomes love.

EMBRACE

What do your eyes whisper to the swift birds
from distant shores?
Invisible in clover
the star-filled night flickers on your lips.

You ask me why do I point my hand to the west.
I tremble lucent in the beauty of the dusk
and only with the unmistakable downward stride
I disguise the anguish of the naked flower.

You console me with a smile
which, dazzling, throws a dark green shadow
on the deserted lake.

The evening is golden red and so like the existent world.
The birds keep flying over us
pensively.
In gentle shores the day extends into the unknown.

SLAVERY

1957

HOME ON THE ROAD

I was lying in the dust by the road.
Neither did I see his face
nor did he see mine.

The stars descended, and the air was blue.
Neither did I see his hands
nor did he see mine.

The East became green as a lemon.
I opened my eyes for a bird.

Then I realized whom I loved
all my life.
Then he realized whose miserable hands
he was embracing.

And the man took his bundle and
departed for his home crying.
But his home is the dust on the road
just as is mine.

SLAVERY

I am a woman. My confession too old and dark
trembled unuttered
before the immobile consciousness of the hills.
Stop, stars,
while I sing this truthful hymn
about a slave and a woman and an eagle
that flew up into the azure.

I loved the most beautiful lads
in this valley and in all the valleys
through which flow rivers, and dreams, and suns.
If you knew how I loved them
you would cry. If you knew how I kept vigil at their side
you would never sleep peacefully
beside a woman nor beside a forest
nor beside vagabonds' fire.

I loved them as a scientist loves an unknown region
to which he sets off, followed by no one.
There is not a marsh I didn't cross
nor a tree before which I did not fall
nor a hill toward which I did not raise my eyes
seeking salvation.

Love was stronger than I.
My body trembled
touching happiness, like an open road
that shrinks far into the distance.

Oh, you who waste tears
on each separation, on each flower
on each circle that disappears in the water,
you who protect your thighs for the most excruciating pain
and remain humiliated before fate
help me, to utter the vanity of radiance
the dust of beauty that covers us.
The burden of truth, under which we broke
carrying it devotedly, as if we carry irresistible fruit
of our dark womb. As if we carry
a lit torch of life.

I am not wiser than you. My road
is the same as that of a water carrier
who cannot escape the steep wall of the well
and in rest doesn't decrease her servitude.
Look at my shoulders. Scars
on them are similar to yours.
And wrinkles around my lips
are bitter from years of patience
and from wormwood of silence.

Don't close the windows, maidens!
This is your voice too, the voice
of a frightened night that scorns
its slavery, and wants to become an eagle.
Come out to the streets, and you will see
as I kneel before each doorstep
at which knelt a Woman.

Not one of you has been
as obedient as I.
And not one of you has so defiantly
and indignantly lifted your face,
and looked up above the tops of juniper trees
at the eagles
and at the sky.

Oh, what is it to me to lose one wing, one eye,
what is it to me to give up several springs
several water wells, and the best harvests
which will never again return!

What is it to me to forget the grass
of my childhood and the town of my youth.
I was devoted to the tree of love.
And I cried when in a storm the wind would
shake the crowns of the trees.

Love was stronger than I.
And the man was a temple
with a golden façade of my dreams
on the pillars of my modesty.

While he slept, I tiptoed down to the
doorstep, and lay down on the stone
covering myself with moist stars.
And when he got up, I pitied his hands
equally tired when they earn bread
and when they carry weapons and flags.

I was saying that the night
had not yet touched my youth.
And I hid my tears, so he would believe me.

And when they recognized in my eyes a smile
with which a woman gives herself forever
to the one with whom she will share the secret,
they turned their face from me,
and looked somewhere into the distance
jealous at the freedom
of high-flying birds
that chose the solitary view
and renounced the sweet valleys
which they themselves could not renounce.

And they hugged me inattentively
and irritably. And they undressed me
as a criminal, not as a woman.
And these feet trampled upon me, these hands beat me,
these lips ridiculed the kisses.
But I continued to smile
persistently and innocently. I loved them.
I told them they were dear and wise
and I hid the tears, so they would believe me.

Then they caressed me
as kings caress their favourite slave.
But I felt in their hands
the burning glow of the whip. And in their voice
the howling of the wolves in the wilderness.

I swear upon my youth, here I have witnesses,
the dust of this road and this well
whose deep waters I conjured.
When I looked at them, they were wolves.
It was, in fact, wilderness and night.
And I only a prey, lured before the cave
into the burrow of a sensualist, at the feet of a conqueror.

And they continued to look peacefully
at some golden spot in the sky, which was ascending,
and after which, I think, was that eagle
that was circling above the valleys.

And when they completely believed
in my closeness and my steadfastness,
I looked in the direction they were looking
into the distance blue and luxurious, into the
heights toward which soar only the brave.
And I wished that I were that golden bird,
the wingspread eagle in the midst of the sky.

Then I began to laugh.
I was opening the door wide and I laughed, I laughed
over the grass and wheat stacks,
to the dark wind-barren earth
with which they girded my strength.

And my laughter awoke at dawn
and dissipated until the first stars.
And then I fell asleep tired
as if from crossing a hill.

I was wondering about that perfidious traveller
who stopped his horse
under this hill, on this sand.
And seeks a night's lodging at the doorstep of a woman.
And wants me to sing him a lullaby,
I, who will scorn tenderness
in order to reach my own truth.
I, whose tomorrow's longing
I already read in the flight of the lost bird.

And I turned my face
not to see desire on his.
And I stopped laughing.

And crying stealthily I left. I left completely certain.
I left on a sad road, to be a singer of wanderings.

To no longer search, no longer believe.

I don't believe in the virtue of the master.
I remember how hands become whips
and how terrible is the embrace
when the conquerors rest
and in whose thankful voice
again is heard the howling of the wolves.

That is why, lads from my valley,
don't believe me when I lie by your side in the grass
meek and obedient as a doe.
Neither when I am nurturing and pampering you
nor when I seek your faithfulness

in return for a high spring cloud,
for the storms of my changeable heart.

Pity the one who believes me
and who brings his herd
before my tent, to nurture it!

I will desert him
in the hour when darkness envelopes the fields.
I will straighten my posture
and shake off the flowers with which you decorated me.

And I will tremble, because a tree in the distance
is magnificent, but your love is worthless.
And your flames before the fire of the dawn
are weak and melancholy.

Go your way, lovesick!
My music is not for your ear!
Love was stronger than I.
But the song became an eagle
and it's leaving its valley.

Eagles are flying toward the azure mountains
and they are not turning around.

This is a confession of a woman and a slave.
A song, a foamy wave
curbed by the sun.

OUR CHILDHOODS ARE RESPONSIBLE
FOR EVERYTHING

We grew up alone as plants.
And now we have become explorers
of the neglected parts of imagination
unaccustomed to obedience to evil.

We sprung up by the roads
and together with us grew our fear
of wild hoofs which will trample us
and of border rocks which will separate
our youth.

Not one of us has two whole hands.
Two untouched eyes. And a heart
in which a cry has not been hushed.

The world was entering us inharmoniously
and it was wounding our brows
with the clanking of its deadly truths
and the clamor of belated stars.

We are aging. The tales go along with us
as a flock that follows a bonfire in the distance.
And our songs are just as we
burdensome and sad.

A SONG ABOUT SAILORS, STREETS AND NIGHT

Into the dark harbour entered a ship, like a tree
full of resin into its black forest.
From the high bow there descend indolently
those who are accustomed to descend
more sluggishly, into the dark landscape
of unknown life.

And they now go along the shore and sing
those who will be forgotten by all the eyes of the world.
Those whom the ocean saw exiled
in a dreadful masculine form, and heard
their blood as it roars
toward the empty night in revolt of its own sun.

The black tree of the sea! The green hurricane
above the crowns of invisible deserts!
Thirst and hunger of love roam tonight
down your streets, expanded city!

How shall I look into the cruel pupils
of half-awakened herds that in the dusk
come out of red tents
and seek some invented wellspring
in the shade of the narrow street
where the prostitutes' hands flutter as yellow sunflowers?

Who am I, to eavesdrop this night on
the cry of the wind, the sailors' nostalgia,

and the old lament of the tavern that leaves
its corner and goes out after happiness?

Who am I, to look at their fingers
as they break bread and to sneak
around their tables, smiling
neither at their story nor at their song. Believing
neither evil nor good? Only suspecting
in each of them a hill
under which, as if under a burden of death, is hidden
the most gentle distant desire.

Am I the sister they sold,
the mother whom they disgraced,
first love from whom they ran
or the last, before whom they will,
crushed, bend their shoulders
and with a smile seek kindness?

Am I the one whom they disrobe
to find in her stature a flower
out of some ancient and lush yearning
transplanted onto that naked island
of icy algae?

The one who smiles while she is pursued
by the soldier's footsteps down the alley
already full of roaming leaves
and the voice of the lost rain?

She who puts false jewels
on her forehead, and appears before the hunters
so they drive foolish deer
into the trap of her throat, at midnight
of the snowy glow, toward the frozen
fiords of sleep. Into the spaciousness
of white strength, that will become a tear?

Am I the one you seek
under the lamp of embankments, at dawn
to thrust a curse into her breast
and leave forever, mocking
her thin hands that wave
naively, and her sad imagination
that still grieves about childhood?

Am I the sea that rocks you
on its wave, the hill that calls you
to its darkness, the night cloud
which sticks cutting edges of lightning bolts
into your living flesh? Because having taken
your scream with me, I traverse
lands and horizons, carrying somewhere
a hoarse exultation of satiated love.

Am I, oh sailors, brothers,
that sole pain for which you yearn?
The darkest of all pains like the earth
opened up by an earthquake, like a sword
halved into two. The blue body
into which you enter like into a sound of a gong

from the other side of the river, and you don't hear
how the valleys are continuously wounded.

Or am I, my brothers,
that woman with crying eyes
who nurses your infants religiously
as if with her milk she saves a century
from continual and enormous suffering? From suffering
which we didn't deserve, but which
our time calls the suffering of mankind!

I know both secrets. Both wings
under which you retreat noble
and dejected. The one and the other
wing of sorrow. The one and the other
loneliness.

You speak, and your muttering
already hushed becomes a prayer.
But my ear hears your peace
among the uproar of the world. And while you cry
on my breasts, and while I rock
your overflowing youth at my pedestal
of moonlight, whispering to you
something soothing and as like autumn shore,
I nevertheless listen continuously to the throws
into the distant gong, and I converse
with the darkness of the world about its fate
uncertain but already present
behind the foggy folds of the hills.

Tomorrow when you return to your homeland
and arrive before your home, at the doorstep
I shall again stand serious
beside your daughters in my hands full of soot
and soil. Black woman
with cried-out eyes. The black trail
of your life, that remained behind you
on the blue elevation of youth.

That, there, will again be I who receive you
smiling, on my bed
cold and clean as the bed
in a wellspring amidst the moss.

Sailors, brothers, look at me!
I am just like you – inconstant sand
under the inconstant sky. A meek traveller
who above the brow has an olive branch
and by the bedstead self-denial.

I am only the face of the world
and I cannot reach you. I pass by you
as by a fortress
into which fertility is walled.

Look: there, from out of the black forest
sailed out a dark tree
and it set sail for the uneasy landscape
of an unknown life.

Greetings to you, tree of the sea!
Greetings to you deserts
in my lap, regions of loneliness.

The night doesn't know to whom to take our call.
The day will not know how to protect us
from the voice of the night that follows us.

All our ships are unveiled.
Sailors, brothers: We are the same!

You and Never

1959

NEVER

I don't know where the emptiness of the sea begins.
But I suspect that in you or in me there touched a voice
which somewhere near said:
never.

That's a river that no longer returns
to its source
because her shores have an agreement with someone unknown
who waits in the distance.

That's a flower that no longer descends
to its root
because there settled the future.

Never.
Murmuring grass of the untrampled plateaus,
snow on the purple
mountains.

Turn behind you and look at your own Never
grown in the grass of hearing and sight
in the shade of exhausted hands, in the radiance of unextinguished
desire.

Look around, recognize your own Never
spread about the vanished lowlands.
And the oppressive thought which you have brought up
will become gentle, because next to it is a man
incomprehensible in his own solitude.

But when he moves into the Night
and into the great restful expanse,
you'll extend after him your hands
and shout:
don't leave!

GOLD

If life is a river that flows
love is gold that settled on the bottom.
The river rocks it in its bed.
And the gold grows. And the longer
the river carries it, the more golden it becomes.

I have travelled over three lowlands.
The roar of the spring is far behind me
and where the mouth of the river hides I do not know.
But when I look at the bottom
clear gold shines in the gravel.
And from the high stalks of summer
my gold is even more magnificent.

THE MURMUR OF THE WINGS
AND THE MURMUR OF THE WATER

We walked along the brink. On one side was night
and on the other water.

The night wanted to show us the regions
where man and bird easily stray,
if the man does not believe the bird
nor the bird believes the man.

The water had so much to tell us
about its long experience, in its
everyday association with man.

But we were going carefree
past the water and the night.

Not one of us suspected their own
distressing face: that renewal
of silence of the plants. The aging of the sun.

The stones lay about like strewn summer metal.

At dusk
the hills in the distance moved apart
and again drew together.

Three wild ducks overtook the river.
And hiding in the light of the faded sun
transformed into the countryside peace
where the dawn was beginning.

Out of the night appeared a silhouette of the windy hill.
And I think: How far
has love drifted.

Love without remembrance is a naked branch
on which birds do not descend.
The thought continuously wants its immortal radiance.

Let the tree push forth leaves in the wind, let the green branch
blossom in my heart.

Love has drifted far.

The world which approaches us whispers to us silhouettes
of forest trees on the horizon
that grow out of bent shadows.

Sit on the threshold
and wait
until the evening moves on.

In the end everyone is again alone with their strangeness.
The travellers have lost recollection
of true homeland, and frightened call each other
by unknown names.

Let's hold back the shadows and listen to the echo.

Days fly off on the wings of swallows.

I must still weave twelve green baskets.
(I forgot the word to which you respond from sleep.)

There is silence and uneasiness
as if we were here for years.

When I think about you, I am summer
with green rain in an old forest.
My breasts are full of seagrass.
Your voice is perhaps for me
an unknown source.
Your name is the flag which flutters on
a fortress and doesn't allow me to fall asleep.

Long since wavering
we descended here and placed our burden
into the lap of the sea.

We poured oil into the old lamp
which was burning neglected
with an unsteady flame.
And we began to listen
to the sound of gravel rolling
and to the murmur of the foam fading.

O, water of the black mouth.
Sea, the roaring year of salt,
there is no peace in your solitude.

When he was leaving, I saw in his eyes
one thought, gone astray
like a precious stone in the sand of a desert.

I knew: he is lost.

He passed through me like a wave
touching those who sleep
in the mountain of unstirred winds.

He flew by like an echo
through my cliffs.

He fell like snow
on my wings

and transformed into silence.

Let's stop for a moment in front of the quiet water.
Look: now we are imprisoned
in our eyes
and in our separation.

Your voice heavy like the smell of burned plants.
While we spoke
the grass perhaps heard us
or the night
smothered by the meadow.

The scenery is a momentary reliance on shadows.

Three times during the night the way was blocked
and who is to find a stone thrown
by a tired hand into the river that flows
in the quick river of blended waves.

Ancient river, forget!
Continue the path through the naked willows
remembering your own or our
suffering.

A Coral Returned to the Sea

1959

A CORAL RETURNED TO THE SEA

I am returning this scarlet hoop of sun, this star of the earth in the
    mirror of the sea,
embodied sight of life which cannot be uprooted, which grows
in the colony of live marine roots and large, immobile fish.
I am returning what I took at the beginning to decorate myself like
    a plant for the celebration of people and spring
before the morning icon of light and winds from afar,
I am returning the seed of life, this red branchlike flower
that is neither stone nor shell nor salt nor vine nor seed
but lives and grows and can become a mountain in the center of
    the ocean.
I am returning my youth and my death and everything that a tree
    made from morning to night,
I am returning sails to the high seas and birds to the land,
creeks to clover, nests to chests of light in the east,
tenderness to the bitter and confused, courage to those assembled
    for departure,
solitude to the stray moon, sadness to the herds from the mountain
    dawn,
I am returning a cradle to the sea, I am separating the fire into two
    flint-stones
and I am continuing to tread down untrodden roads of my life
which is taken over by the march of the stars and the abundance
    of silence.

A SONG TO THE STAIRS THAT DESCEND
INTO THE LEAVES

I did not tell you that through this town and any other and who
    knows when
runs a gilded river, all with deep-brown leaves.
It comes to us with the silence of a cloud, and returns by a devastated
    forest
in autumn most remote.

In this city you and I live, full of fear of what has passed.
Because of the night which from us becomes heavy
and near us descends the stairs
aging as a tall bare tree.

Quietly, as if it is necessary for the trees
we move apart. As if it is good
not for us, but for the long thought-out design
of this city. For autumn which will take the leaves down its own path.

Perhaps the pain will become free and depart for where the birds go
if it is true that they go, and we stay.
If it is true that we shall once lose everything
having stored in ourselves the gold of the leaves.

A BALLAD ABOUT SUNRISE

The sun gilded the tips of the mountains.
From the sea rises a restless morning wind.
Deep down in the fishing bay
sleeps the dark green of olive trees.

The people of my homeland go one after another
in the moist voices the spring already separates.
They climb into the fields with their small burros
which still tremble beaten by the dew of the leaves.

The people of my homeland have serious faces.
Their tools of labor shimmer with an unpolished shine.
Oh, my friends, stop so I can ask you
about what the sea thinks in its persistent distant reflection

The sullen pines fade on the rock.
From the sea rises the restless morning wind.
Every dawn the oil from the quiet olive groves
cries out desolate with the sadness of dark clouds.

The people of my homeland go one after another
sadness sleeps in them as an ancient echo.
The bleats of the sheep roam among the wild grasses.
The seagulls shriek under the sheer rocks.

The sun gilded the tips of the mountains.
I lie in the silence of the deep bay.
The branches of old olives, touched by the wind,
rustle near the empty sea with their long and bitter murmur.

A ROCK ON WHICH A BALLAD OUGHT TO BE ENGRAVED

Let it be known that we haven't always been sad:
there is a moment when love and life become one.
In a black stone one can decipher the earth's dream.
In a drop of rain on a leaf of the sullen fig tree
the celebration of summer could last for centuries
and the sun would never descend
behind the bare shrivelled hills.

In one single name as in an old prayer
hides the unhappy and the quiet sense of the world.
As it becomes paler, peace too has gone.
The heart cannot build it again.
And the thought is unable to search for it
in the hatred of things that dispute one another.

Time, why do you let us measure you
with our forehead that has ceased to yearn?
Love, we also measured you
with a false scale of the wavering world.

ALAS! MORNING
1963

ACCURSED RAIN
1969

A BIRD

I close my eyes, the invisible bird sings

Having collected a myriad of sun drops into one
It tries to explain again everything that we once
Called in her name
Life
(She did not agree with that
And sings
To warn us about the unknown mistake)

Everything we know about ourselves can fit forever
Into her obedient silver body

Her neck is a vase turned toward the treetops

But life is nevertheless that about which no one sings
That which we protected and left to overtake us

At sunset
When we will
Silently
Leave
The same bird will again sing the same song, the same hill
Presence is not expended, it is incomparable

The sojourn between the two moist rings chirps
Only the inexperienced grimace of anticipation
Is on the fluctuating wall of the morning where the big bell-clapper
Of a clock, of a golden bird, accelerates the day

JANUARY

From my outer side strikes the winter morning
Like the wind upon a broken drum
From my alien side from my most solitary side
Someone's palm someone's fingers
Attempt in vain to make me
Insensitive to my truth
To my perpetual summer of green dams
To the mesmerizing noon song of the frogs

From my outer side strikes the winter morning
From my inner side ripens a vineyard
So solitary so blue
Like the waters that never die
Like glaciers wine and echo

The waters that never die
And that leave nothing behind them

From my inner side scratch the frozen
Nails of trees of the inaudible beast of spring

A GRAIN OF EMOTION

I awake and whisper: love, be a song,
then I will live with you, giving you to the people.
And the people will return to me something from your leaves
when they go out for a stroll
through the streets
washed in rain.
Is there such a town where trees do not die
is there such tenderness one can reach
secretly
on some long, long
white staircase?

I was good like summer and slender
with thick tresses.
I was magnificently good. I was like summer.
I am not ashamed to say this; anyway, it is now
autumn.
Goodness lies below leaves and its smile is
invisible.
I was a forest. I was good like summer
and slender, with thick tresses.
And what has remained? This: a grain of emotion in the pupils.
I awake and whisper:
love, be a song!

ASHAMED TO DIE

1974

HOLIDAY OF BLINDNESS

If we had true eyes, if we had not been born blind,
We would see around us neither landscape nor plum orchards
We would see how the city ages, how the wind dies
We would see how amongst themselves rules of a game interchange
How essence touches essence, thought movement.
We would see a man asleep on the palm of a huge plant
Which carries him through the night, which disentangles his shadow.
We would see ourselves not *surrounded* by others: but split
By their short orbit through our airy flesh.
We would see ourselves in the mirror already ingrown to the core in
    others
As we look at the storm, so we would look, erect,
At the deeply moving play of reciprocity, in which we ourselves are
    involved.
If the old bell-towers had eyes, how embarrassed would be
Our nonexistent *I*
And it would fall on its knees.

BECAUSE OF YOU

Because of you, not because of me, now in me occurs
this blossoming of crystal petals. A call
heard nowhere, but present everywhere.
Arrested wings of solitude
lay down between us and wait for
the moment to unfold again.

A kiss: a sharp thrust into the heart. As a taste
of wild pineapple. Darkness and old women
who descend cobblestone stairs
with a bundle of seasons under their arms

and who don't look if there is anyone on the road.

But we stand next to the evergreen and know
this sad evening is unrepeatable.

Look, a white swan on the water. A puzzle.
The eye only grazes it, and only puts it
in its dark treasury
because of you.

ALONE WITH THESE FLOWERS

The day was, as usual, everybody's.

Everyone had in it a part of oneself –
the most concealed smile emerged like a seed,
drawn by the light, on the quiet surface
of a region which had always
expected it.

The day, as usual, was gathering from our faces
powdered gravel, the mute remains of
long uttered words in the murmur of sleep

intended perhaps for someone in the woods

who suddenly became so close to us
and unreachable. The brook
full of silver frozen birds, discarded voices
of old leaves, rushes through a thin twilight
toward the other hill
and another trill of wind
enveloped in our hard
shadows.

The day was, as usual, everybody's.
And it was easy to recognize in it
that which belongs to us, by affinity
between the fluttering weave of the inner
and the outer sky.

That radiance of movement
of time, since we have adopted it for ourselves
and from it made our soul; since we have
deposited our soul into the silence
of departing flowers, here we are now
before you, incomprehensible
nothingness.

I, alone with these flowers
and the world from the other side of touch by the azure waters
unresolved with itself, incessantly
strange to our eyes. And innocent.

Love.
From out of the sunset's forehead come wounded birds.
I, alone with these flowers of the night

Love: only migration, migration...

LULLABY

On my hands sleeps
spring, like a lamb.
White pathways
ran out of the woods.

The moon's sickle
pushed aside the branches.
The stars inaudibly
sat upon the grass.

The leaves of grass
softly rustled
and weaved for the sky
a blue bed.

THE SECRET OF THE YELLOW AFTERNOON

My cat is sad.
I cannot decipher
her loneliness;
these tales she has purred
in some obsolete
drawer of her being.

Yesterday it seemed to me
that I shall always love her.
The sky was grey
and someone was walking down
a long green street
scattering stones.
She was listening
attentively and intensely.
It seemed to her, I think,
that someone was crying
far in the third yard
and she looked scared.

And I remembered someone
who has never cried
and who has never
overheard
the pain of mankind.
And I was ashamed
of that worn-out recollection
because of which the shadows
on the wall began to cry.

And the cat lay down
in the coal basket
and she did not want
to know anything more.
And again I saw
everything in its place:
the street became
gloomy and wet
and the clock in the tower
whispered to the fire
which was dozing
one more tale.
And here I sit defenceless
and so close
to this ancient intimacy
between the cat and the tower
and I cannot decipher
anything in it
except loneliness
that penetrates to the bone.

Well, now I am that
defenceless being
who pricks up its ears
and listens intensely
as someone in the yard
moans more softly
and the yellow afternoon
moves on beyond redemption.

THE APPROACH OF SPRING

The wind of spring, the wind of spring
the wind of solitude
the wind
of sunlight

The wind
oh, you
who are not alive
but who reveal
life

*

Tell me, my wall,
how is called
this freshly scattered
blue looking glass

Is this the sky
or flown off
soul of winter
a freed
raven

*

The wind.
I fear
its steps
which are departing

Its hands
still completely cold
and coarse from frost
among the purple
branches

*

Someone will embrace me
I will fall asleep.
Someone will leave
I will die.

I will never again
be in love
with something transient
with something
that cries

So pass by me
pass quickly
green dew of March
fire of spring

*

I wish to walk
in a spring evening
follow the dusk
across the meadow
ashamed that I am leaving
perhaps forever
and not knowing anything more
about myself or about you

That is how ashamed winter is
when it abandons the trees
in which it spent the winter
hiding squirrels

*

I wish to leave
leave alone
greeting the good
big sun
which rises slowly
from the other side of eyes

With a taste of the first
flowers on the lips
longing for a summer of fish
on deserted shores
a wellspring of green
in the starlit
bosom

*

Let everything grow
grow and ache!
Let the blade of grass
be happy at the swaying
of its shadow

Oh, the blade of discovery
unrepeatably bitter!
Let the mystery and miracle
smile at me.
I wish to fall asleep
kissing that reality
which deceived me
which tempted me
forward into a day
a day nontransparent

*

To die while walking
cuddled by the leaves
in a surge of sleep
swollen from gazing

Oh, let death be
that clearest apparition
serenely flawless
love and longing

As if I enter
into the endless sea
of desire

As if I emerge
naked
out of snowy lake

*

Let this stone in the bosom
radiate warmth.
I wish to die believing
in the words at which
I tremble.

Lean against me
white miners.
You can come out
from your black hoops
wash your hands
and sit beside
the cradle.

And I leave because of you
tillers in the furrows
you who have become
small like grains

This music of the wind
and the earth I will scatter
believing in myself
and in everything that kept
wounding me

*

Spring, pull out
of my heart the knife!
I kept calling winter
not to pluck it out too soon
and I implored autumn
not to touch it

Who thrusted it there
please, trees
and clouds, have mercy!
Pull out, pull out
the knife from my heart

*

Spring, a big forest hedgehog
walks together with its
prickly shadow
from brink to brink
of this thin
surface of the world
spattered with sunlight.

What was this body doing
naked in the crack
among germs and graves
graves and germs?

*

I want to grow
corpses, where are you?
I too want to grow
to stretch my arms
to spread my wings

What do you bring me, spring,
except melancholies
of purple towns
and silver puddles
in the outskirts, near a bridge
with huge arches
and pillars that ache

*

Look, the hands are immobile
and everything is puzzling.
The breasts are sleeping
and the blood is resting.

Spring, invent for me
this time something mild.
Bring me a gift
deep like a lake.

*

Now is my holiday
I was born in spring
together with you, willows,
and with you the homeless
the nameless, faithful
to a nameless obligation.

Bring me eternal
friendship
with the earth

And of these who look
through the seams of the earth
let no one respond
to me anymore.

Perhaps only the old
old gardener
of winter
and all who in vain
love life.

I am waiting for you, river.
Let us depart on a new road!

*

I know, a red apple is
decaying on the window.
December flowers
are rotting in the room.
The sunlight squints
and the days are toothless.
They need a blue shield
forged.
Black crutches
painted green.

The gravedigger is impatient.
Hurry, spring!

*

Hurry, spring!
Many dark rooms
await you to strike
against the brass jug.
Enter!

Look, here children are
born with a smile
which rusts in the rain

as soon as a cloud
appears.
Don't lie to them.
Tell them the whole truth.
Today there are no flowers
today is not a holiday.

*

Today begins the ancient
unknown world.
The forgotten battle
hurts once again.
Bread left on the table
turned black, turned black.
Turned black from years
turned black from thirst.

*

I found in a drawer
the remains of some ship.
An old glove
in a glass noose.
A jar long ago overturned
became silence.
How can I disrupt
this order
with my departure?

*

Departure is disorder
departure is rapture
departure is doubt
in everything around us

In our birth
akin to the wind.
Drops possess us
dust doesn't love us

Departure is love.
Departure is that
final what we have.
Our golden key.
It is good that we have it.

*

We were crying. It is good
we admit that to someone.
Perhaps to you, spring?
Perhaps again to you
while we totter through our homeland
from corner to corner
from ash to shadow
from a star to an apparition
carrying this bit
of eternity in ourselves.

Yes. This bit
of eternity
which sings.

Sofia, February 1967.

EPILOGUE

I shall never be
a prickly grass
and black robbers
will not tread upon me.
Everything I once
gave to this sky
time will return to me
with each of its
birds.
I shall never be
a trampled grass
and I will rustle clearly
so the children
understand me.
Who passes by me
will be happy.
And the bell, the old sinner,
will cease to toll.

Translator's Note

Several poems from this collection appeared recently in the powerful monodrama under the title *I, Who Have Hands More Innocent*, written by Vesna Parun and Vesna Tominac Matačić. The monodrama focuses on the turbulent life and work of the Croatian poet Vesna Parun. In 2016, during the month-long performances at the Fringe Festival in Edinburgh, Scotland, several very positive reviews appeared in print. In one such review by Lucian Waugh for the *Exeunt Magazine*, he applauds the "revelatory existential meditations of extraordinary power and insight" that Parun's poetry reveals throughout the performance. In addition, he bemoans the fact that the original 1985 edition of the book is out-of-print. It is this commentary which served as an impetus to bring out a new edition of *Selected Poems of Vesna Parun*.

Though it is impossible to render in translation the sound patterns of the original language, I have attempted to preserve the tone of the original voice, and to stay as close as possible to the original meaning. It is important to keep in mind that, while crossing the bridge from one language to another, the *how* may wander and be lost, but it is the *what* that I tried to make sure is not lost in translation.

I am grateful to Vesna Tominac Matačić and the whole Zagreb Actor's Studio for reviving interest in Vesna Parun whose work captured my interest in bringing it to print for the first time in English translation. The intent of this new edition is to bring this extraordinary poet, writer, translator, and artist to the attention of the new generation of readers.

About the Poet

Vesna Parun was born on April 10, 1922, on the island of Zlarin near Šibenik on the Dalmatian coast in Croatia. She began writing poetry as a child, publishing her first poem "Spring" in 1932 in the magazine *Guardian Angel*. After finishing high school in Split, she moved to Zagreb where in 1940 she began attending the University of Zagreb studying Romance languages. World War II interrupted her studies to which she returned in 1945, focusing on philosophy. While on a work brigade, she contracted typhus and dropped her studies. In 1947, Parun made her literary debut with the publication of a collection of poems entitled *Zore i vihori (Dawns and Hurricanes)*. The following year her second collection of poems *Pjesme (Poems)* appeared in print, and, afterwards, she devoted herself exclusively to writing. During her lifetime Vesna Parun authored and published more than seventy books, among which are collections of poetry, prose, drama, essays, children's books, satirical poems, and translations of poetry from Bulgarian, French, German, and Slovenian. Her own writing has been translated into a dozen world languages. In addition to writing, Vesna Parun engaged in painting and drawing artwork, which was displayed in a number of exhibits. The main themes of her art are linked to nature.

Poet, prose writer, critic, translator, and artist, Vesna Parun spent the last decade of her life in Special Hospital in Stubičke Toplice outside Zagreb, from where she published a number of her last works. After her death on October 25, 2010, she was interred in the grave of her ancestors on the island of Brač, Croatia. Recipient of a number of literary awards, she is the first woman in Croatia who lived for and by writing.

ABOUT THE TRANSLATOR

Dasha C. Nisula taught Russian and Croatian languages, literature, and culture. She is a translator of poetry and short stories from these languages, and the author of four books, numerous articles, reviews, and translations. Her work has appeared in *An Anthology of South Slavic Literatures*, and the literary journals *Modern Poetry in Translation, Southwestern Review, International Poetry Review,* and *Massachusetts Review,* among others. She is a member of the American Literary Translators Association, living and working in Kalamazoo, Michigan.

ABOUT THE ARTIST

Marko Marian is an Instructor of Art at Anoka-Ramsey Community College in Cambridge, Minnesota. His art has been shown and collected throughout the United States. Marian's landscape paintings and drawings focus on human mediation of local sites and, more recently, on the multigenerational experience of Croatian immigrants on Minnesota's Iron Range.

ACKNOWLEDGEMENTS

Almost all of the poems in this book were selected from *Šum krila, šum vode* (*The Murmur of the Wings, the Murmur of the Water*), edited with an afterword by Branko Maleš, Zagreb: Mladost, 1981. The last six poems are from the collection *Stid me je umrijeti* (*Ashamed to Die*), selected and edited by Vlatko Pavletić, Zagreb: Mladost, 1989.

The editors of the following periodicals deserve acknowledgement for publishing some of these poems before and after this book was printed.

Journal of Croatian Studies, Vol. XXIII, 1982, pp. 43-69. Poems: "You with Hands More Innocent," "Slavery," "A Song About Sailors, Streets and Night," "A Ballad About Sunrise," and "January."

International Poetry Review, Vol. IX, No. 2, Fall, 1983, pp. 68-69. Poems: "I am Not a Woman" and "And Then There Was that Tree."

Cross Currents: A Yearbook of East European Culture, No. 10, 1991, pp. 125-126. Poems: "A Return to the Tree of Time" and "Sleeping Youth."

An Anthology of Croatian Literature, Edited by Henry R. Cooper, Jr. Bloomington, IN: Slavica Publishers, 2011, pp. 223-225. Poems: "First Love," "A Rock on Which a Ballad Ought to Be Engraved," and "A Grain of Emotion."

I wish to thank Elizabeth Marquart for typing and commenting on the English text for the second edition, Dillon Dolby for his technical skills in putting all the parts of this project together, and Dr. Roxanne Panicacci for her suggestions on the final draft. For preparing the illustrations, I am indebted to Marko Marian, Anoka-Ramsey Community College, Cambridge, Minnesota. This second edition is being published with the support from the Provost, College of Arts and Sciences, and the Department of World Languages and Literatures at Western Michigan University. In addition, I would like to thank Michael Callaghan, Publisher of Exile Editions, for his interest in putting this work to print.

D.C.N.

Zore i vihori / Dawns and Hurricanes. Lyrics. Zagreb: Croatian Writers' Association, 1947.

Pjesme / Poems. Zagreb: Matica hrvatska, 1948. (Matica Hrvatska Award)

Crna maslina / Black Olive Tree. Lyrics. Zagreb: Croatian Writers' Association, 1955. (City of Zagreb Award)

Vidrama vjerna / Faithful to Otters. Lyrics. Zagreb: Zora, 1957.

Ropstvo / Slavery. Lyrics. Belgrade: Nolit, 1957.

Pusti da otpočinem / Let Me Rest. Lyrics. Sarajevo: Narodna prosvjeta, 1958.

Ti i nikad / You and Never. Lyrics. Zagreb: Lykos, 1959.

Koralj vraćen moru / A Coral Returned to the Sea. Lyrics. Zagreb: Naprijed, 1959. ("Vladimir Nazor" Award)

Marija i mornar / Mary and the Sailor. Drama performed in Zadar and Zagreb, 1959-1961.

Konjanik / The Horseman: Selected poems. Arranged by Karmen Milačić. Zagreb: Školska knjiga, 1962.

Jao jutro / Alas! Morning. Lyrics. Belgrade: Prosveta, 1963.

Bila sam dječak / I was a Boy. Selected poems. Zagreb: Naprijed, 1963.

Potres u gradiću Kale / Earthquake in the Town of Kale. Drama manuscript 1964, not presented.

Vjetar trakije / The Wind of Thrace. Lyrics. Zagreb: Zora, 1964.

Pjesme / Poems. Selected with an Afterword by V. Krmpotić. Zagreb: Matica hrvatska, 1964.

Gong / A Gong. Lyrics. Zagreb: Naprijed, 1966.

Otvorena vrata / Opened Door. Selected poems. Belgrade: Prosveta, 1968.

Ukleti dažd / Accursed Rain. Lyrics. Zagreb: Zrinski, 1969.

Apsirt, Medejin brat / Apsirt, Medea's Brother. A tragedy in three acts, presented in 1969.

Karpatsko umiljenije: Tragom Magde Isanos / Carpathian Ingratiation: In Footsteps of Magda Isanos. Sonnets from Romania with Radomir Andrić. Kruševac: Bagdala, 1971.

Penjo Penev, Poezija / Penjo Penev, Poetry. Poems translated from the Bulgarian by V. Parun. Zagreb: Mladost, 1971.

Sto soneta / One Hundred Sonnets. Lyrics. Čakovec: Zrinski, 1972.

I prolazim životom / And I Am Passing Through Life. Lyrics. Belgrade: Nolit, 1972.

Stid me je umrijeti / Ashamed to Die. Lyrics. Zagreb: August Cesarec, 1974.

Olovni golub / The Lead Pigeon. Lyrics. Belgrade: Slovo ljubve, 1975.

Apokaliptičke basne / Apocalyptic Fables. Lyrics. Belgrade: Nolit, 1976.

Ljubav bijela kost / Love, a White Bone. Lyrics. Zagreb: Surla, 1978.

Magareči otok / Donkey's Island. Performed at the Croatian National Theater, Zagreb, 1979.

Salto mortale / Somersault. Satirical-autobiographical sonnets. Zagreb: Sveučilišna naklada Liber, 1981.

Šum krila, šum vode / Murmur of Wings, Murmur of Water. Poems selected by Branko Maleš. Zagreb: Mladost, 1981.

Izabrana Djela / Selected Works. Pet stoljeća hrvatske književnosti, #155. Zagreb: Matica hrvatska, 1982.

Pod muškim kišobranom / Under a Man's Umbrella. Sketches, satire, other prose. 1958-1986. Zagreb: Globus, 1987.

Grad na Durmitoru / City on Durmitor. Lyrics. Nikšić: NIO Univerzitetska riječ, 1988.

Poezija. Poetry. Selected and Edited by Marko Vešović. Sarajevo: Veselin Masleša, 1988.

Kasfalpirova zemlja / Kasfalpir Earth. Essay and sonnets, Selected and Edited by Vlatko Pavletić. Zagreb: Mladost, 1989.

Krv svjedoka i cvijet / Blood of the Witness and a Flower. A novel. Selected and Edited by Karmen Milačić. Zagreb: Mladost, 1990.

Nedovršeni mozaik / Unfinished Mosaic. Sketches, essays, etc. Selected and Edited by Karment Milačić. Zagreb: Mladost, 1990.

Indigo grad / Indigo City. Poems in prose. Karlovac: Osvit, 1990.

Sonetni vijenci / Wreaths of Sonnets. Zagreb: Prosvjeta, 1991.

Tronožac koji hoda / Three-legged Who Walks. Satirical poems, epigrams. Zagreb: Znanje, 1993.

Začarana čarobnica / Enchanted Sorceress. Poetry and prose. Zagreb: s.p., 1993.

Kako ili autobiografska buncanja / How or Autobiographical Nonsense. With Moma Dimić. Vršac: Književna opština Vršac, 1994.

Ptica vremena / A Bird of Time. Poetry, prose, drama. Selected and Introduced by Karmen Milačić. Zagreb: Mozaik knjiga, 1996.

Pjesnici druge Moderne / Poets of the Second Modernism. Selected and Edited by Jure Kaštelan and Ante Stamać. Zagreb: A.B.C. Naklada, 1996.

Smijeh od smrti jači / Laughter Stronger Than Death. Poetry and satire. Zagreb: Studentsko kulturno umjetničko društvo "Ivan Goran Kovačić," 1997.

Pelin basne / Wormwood Tales. Zagreb: Naklada Jurčić, 1998.

Hrvatska kraljica / Croatian Queen. Autobiograhical poem in prose. Zagreb: s.p., 1999.

Zagorski četverolist: Magdica / Zagorje Quatrefoil: Magdica. With Biserka Rožanković and Željko Špoljar. Donja Stubica: Kajkaviana, 1999.

Političko Valentinovo / Political Valentine's. Satire, epigrams. Zagreb: s.p., 2000.

Grijeh smrtni satira / Mortal Sin Satire. Lyrics. Zagreb: s.p., 2000.

Noć za pakost: Moj život u 40 vreća / *Night for Spitefulness: My Life in 40 Bags*. Autobiographical prose. Zagreb: Matica hrvatska, 2001.

Mozak u torbi / *Brains in a Handbag*. Zagreb: Stajergraf, 2001.

Da sam brod / *If I Were a Ship*. Zagreb: Mozaik knjiga, 2002.

Đoko i Đokonda: poetsko-satirični kontrapunkt / *Joko and Jokonda: Poetico-Satirical Counterpoint*. Stubičke Toplice: s.p., 2002.

Suze putuju / *Tears Travel*. Sonnets. Zagreb: Studentsko kulturno umjetničko društvo "Ivan Goran Kovačić," 2002. ("Tin Ujević" Award)

Bubnjevi umjesto srca / *Drums Instead of Heart*. Lyrics. Zagreb: Društvo hrvatskih književnika, 2003.

Na rtu kobi / *At the Point of Destiny*. Sonnets. Stubičke Toplice: s.p., 2005.

Topuzina / *Topuzina*. Autobiographical satire. Stubičke Toplice, s.p., 2006.

Bubamarine lepeze / *Ladybug's Fans*. Drama for adults and children. Stubičke Toplice, s.p., 2006.

Viteški zamak / *Knight's Castle*. Translation of Hrista Jasenova's poetry from the Bulgarian. Stubičke Toplice, s.p. 2006.

Tijelo i duh / *Body and Soul*. Lyrics. Stubičke Toplice: s.p., 2007.

Blagoslov kukolja / *Cockle's Blessing*. Epigrams and lyrics. Stubičke Toplice: s.p., 2007.

Taj divni divlji kapitalizam / *That Wonderful Wild Capitalism*. Book I, 2009; Book II. Satirical lyrics. Zagreb: s.p., 2010.

Ja koja imam nevinije ruke / *I, Who Have Hands More Innocent*. An asynchronous selection and arrangement by Vesna Parun. Zagreb: ZORO, November 2010.

Posljednja volja Vesne Parun: Antologija nesretnih sudbina / *Vesna Parun's Last Testament: An Anthology of Unhappy Fortunes*. Denis Derk. Zagreb: V.B.Z., 2012.

OTHER WORKS: CHILDREN'S LITERATURE

Patka Zlatka / Goldy Duck. Book for children, No. 4. Zagreb: Lykos, 1957.

Kornjačin oklop / Turtle's Armor. Tales in verse. Zagreb: Naša djeca, 1958.

Zec mudrijan / Rabbit the Wise. Poems for children. Sarajevo: Svjetlost, 1958.

Tuga i radost šume / Grief and Joy of the Forest. Zagreb: Mladost, 1958.

Mačak Džingiskan i Miki Trasi / Tomcat Gingiskan and Mickey Tracy. Beginning of "Tomcat" novel in verse for children. Zagreb: Spektar, 1968.

Miki Trasi i baba Pim-Bako / Mickey Tracy and Grandma Pim-Bako. Continuation of "Tomcat" novel in verse for children. Zagreb: s.p., 1968.

Mačak na mjesecu / Tomcat on the Moon. Continuation of "Tomcat" novel in verse for children. Zagreb: s.p., 1969.

Miki slavni kapetan / Mickey, a Famous Captain. Continuation of "Tomcat" novel. Zagreb: Školska knjiga, 1970.

Karneval u Kukljici / Carneval in Kukljica. Belgrade: Grafos, 1974.

Poznanstvo sa danima maloga Maksima / Acquaintance With the Days of Little Maxim. Together with Moma Dimić. Belgrade: Beogradski izdavačko-grafički zavod, 1974.

Igre pred oluju / Games before the Storm. Zagreb: Spektar, 1979.

Mačak Džingiskan / Tomcat Gingiskan. Picture book prepared by Drago Kozina. Zagreb: Naša djeca, 1981.

Škola za skitnice / School for Tramps. Performed in Zagreb 1981, 1983.

Bokser / Boxer. One of 12 picture books printed in Latin and Cyrillic, and translated into Slovenian. Zagreb: Naša djeca, 1982-1983.

Vučjak / German Shepherd. Zagreb: Naša djeca, 1982.

Hoću ljutić, neću mak / I Want Buttercup, Not Poppy. Zagreb: Mladost, 1983.

Miki Trasi / Mikey Tracy. Zagreb: Naša djeca, 1983.

Roda u školi: apokaliptičke i nove basne / Stork in School: Apocalyptic and New Tales. Introduced by Ranko Risojević. Banjaluka: Glas, 1988

Pokraj Kupe kad se vrapci skupe / By Kupa River When the Sparrows Gather. Karlovac: Osvit, 1989.

Moj prijatelj šišmiš: izabrane dječje pjesme / My Friend the Bat: Selected Children's Poems. Zagreb: Mladost, 1990.

Kroz prozorčić zime / Through a Little Window of Winter. Zagreb: Velebit-Velegraf, 1995.

Kukljo, Mukljo, Tanana i Glog. Continuation of "Tomcat" novel. Šibenik: Juraj Šižgori , 1997.

Pčela, duga i mlin / Bee, Rainbow and Mill. Rijeka: Adamić, 1997.

Uspavanka za poljubac / Lullaby for a Kiss. Zagreb: Mozaik knjiga, 1997.

Tri morske pustolovke / Three Sea Adventuresses. Continuation of "Tomcat" novel. Zagreb: Mozaik knjiga, 2000.

Morska kočijica / Maritime Coach. Lyrics. Zagreb: Mozaik knjiga, 2001.

Miki Trasi i primadona / Mikey Tracy and The Leading Lady. Zagreb: Profil International, 2003.

Dar mame medvjedice / Mama Bear's Gift. Tale for children in verse. Zagreb: Sretna knjiga, 2004.

Paun vila / Peacock Fairy. Tale in verse. Stubičke Toplice: s.p., 2005.

Sve zbog truta / All Because of Lazybones. Humorous play. Stubičke Toplice: s.p., 2006.

Prizori iz Nenine štale / Scenes from Nena's Stable. Play for children. Stubičke Toplice: s.p., 2008.

Tri bika zlatoroga / Three Golden Horn Bulls. Play for children. Stubičke Toplice: s.p., 2008.

Postolar, Čavličak, Dobričak / Cobbler, Nailpin, Good Fellow. Play for children. Stubičke Toplice: s.p., 2008.

Miki Trasi i hijena Ššš... / Mikey Tracy and Hyena Shshshsh.... Play for children. Stubičke Toplice: s.p., 2009.

AWARDS

Matica Hrvatska Award, 1948 – for *Pjesme / Poems.*

City of Zagreb Award, 1955– for *Crna Maslina / Black Olive Tree.*

"Vladimir Nazor" Award, 1959 – for *Koralj vračen moru / A Coral Returned to the Sea.*

Poet of the Year, 1959 – for Contribution to Poetry.

Poetry Degree, 1970 – Received in Paris, France.

"Zmaj" Award – Matica Srpska, 1972 – for Children's Poetry.

"Vladimir Nazor" Award, 1982 – for Lifetime Achievement in Literature.

Poeta Oliveatus, 1995 – "Croatia rediviva: Ća, Kaj, Što-Baštinski dani" Festival.

"Visoka žuta žita" Charter Award at the Poetry Meetings in Drenovci, 2002 – for Literary Output and Contribution to Croatian Literature.

"Tin Ujević" Award – Association of Croatian Writers, 2003 – for Collection of Sonnets *Suze putuju / Tears Travel.*

Plaque *Goodmorning Sea,* 2003 – for Continuous Contribution to Croatian Literature.

European Award for Poetry, 2010 – from Literary Municipality of Vršac.

ALPHABETICAL INDEX

Page   Title